Preface

Faced in early in 2015 with the task of researching information for the 800th
anniversary celebrations of the signing of the 'Magna Carta' in June 1215,
so much information was gathered about the period
that it seemed a shame not to share this in a short reference book about the period. I
was not new by any means to carrying out research for projects and writing short
documentaries at local level, and have always felt that somewhere deep inside lay a
budding author, so I hope you enjoy and find this book informative and useful.

Research, Credits and Copyrights

1. Pre "Magna Carta" Monarch photos – BBC History Pages
2. Cambridge University timeline and information – Cambridge University Press
3. English Timelines and Information – English and National history societies
4. All other information with intellectual credits and copyrights observed

In the 13th Century 1200 – 1300 England saw a time of great change and advancement in the country, in previous centuries it was ruled by Monarchs with little respect for their people, even the Barons of the land had little say in the countries running, and were in constant dispute over this.

But by some intellectuals the 13th century was called "the greatest of all centuries", it saw cultural advancement of enormous importance. In 1209, Cambridge University was founded as a second English educational centre after Oxford. In the early 13th Century, the Dominican and Franciscan friars came to England and soon populated the now flourishing universities.

Within a short space of time, English scholars won great renown throughout Europe. Robert Grosseteste, Roger Bacon, Duns Scotus and William of Ockham were typical representatives of English 13th-century intellectual life, and the court of Henry III was a centre of fine arts and books.

At the beginning of the century though England had seen one of its darkest periods under King John. In 1204, he lost Normandy to the French and he was in direct conflict with Pope Innocent III, who excommunicated the English king. In 1209, he put the realm under interdict, and finally, John had to pay homage to the Pope in 1213 and made England a fief of the Roman Church.

This led to a serious rebellion by the nobility and magnates against the king in the next year. With the signing of the 'Magna Carta' though, in 1215, John acknowledged the constitutional framework of his father Henry II which defined the limits of royal prerogatives.

After King John's death in 1216, his elder son, a nine-year-old boy, was crowned as Henry III. The realm was ruled by William Marshal, Earl of Pembroke until 1219. The king's minority ended in 1227.

We can see then, that prior to the signing of the 'Magna Carta', England was in a state of turmoil, with few laws and no one to police those that existed, rights for the people did not exist, and there were no courts or any such systems of trial, an individual could be jailed at will without the right of a fair trial or representation. These were then repressive times to live in, with excessive taxes by the Monarchs, some of who didn't live in the country, it was little wonder that the people were unsettled with their lot.

The signing of the "Magna Carta", by King John and 25 Surety's on the 15th of June 1215, on a battlefield known as 'Runnymede' was one of the most important documents ever signed in England, and was the beginning of what you may today call 'human rights', (freedom, and democracy), it placed limits on the power of the crown, and ensured people could not be jailed or beheaded without fair trial or hearing.

It was not the first time such a document had been thought of, indeed Henry the 1st had set a precedent on his accession to the throne in 1100, thirty years after the Norman Conquest, when he issued a royal proclamation – the 'Coronation Charter', this was also set as a means of atoning for the past abuse of earlier monarchs, particularly 'William Rufus' his predecessor, who had levied heavy taxes on the people to pay for his crusades, causing great unrest among many, the Coronation Charter even though it was later recognised as a precursor to the 'Magna Carta', was conveniently forgotten about and ignored by future kings and queens for the next century.

It was only after the Archbishop of Canterbury, Stephen Langton, also in long term dispute with King John, dusted off the 113 year old proclamation of Henry I and showed it to the Barons that the idea of a new and improved charter – a 'Great Charter' or "Magna Carta" took hold and was developed.

As you can see then, the "Magna Carta" was signed at a time when there was great civil unrest in England due to the way in which the people had been treated badly by previous ruling monarchs, with heavy taxation to fund the crusades and unjust ruling, it had brought the country to the point of civil war.

At the time the "Magna Carta" was signed, King John had ruled from 1199, he had come to the throne after a turbulent period of personal family disputes. John was born around Christmas time in Oxford in about 1166 or 1167, he was the youngest and favourite son of Henry II, on becoming heir he needed to settle the unrest in England so he could have a steady income from the land.

An ally and personal adviser to John was Hugh of Avalon, Bishop of Lincoln, he had warned John against exercising unjust rule over the people, drawing his attention to a scene from the last Judgment. Hugh is thought to have recommended the king to: 'Fix your mind on their perpetual torment and let your heart dwell on their ceaseless punishment. Thus will you understand, the great dangers incurred by those who for a short time are set over others as rulers, but who by not ruling themselves are tormented by devils forever'. That Bishop Hugh was able to make such a remark illustrates the political importance of the Bishop of Lincoln in England at this time.

Later we look more closely at the link between Lincolnshire and the signing of the 'Magna Carta'. And Lincoln Castle where King John had died of dysentery.

<< Left Lincoln Cathedral

Although this may not have been what King John had seen as a way forward he needed to appease the English People, not to succeed in doing this would have only led to further unrest in the country, for sure he was left with little option but to agree to the signing of the Magna Carter.

But, the "Magna Carta" of June 1215 almost suffered the same demise as the 'Coronation Charter' from 1100, when by August 1215 Pope Innocent had annulled the "Magna Carta" declaring it illegal and having been sealed under duress. The humiliation of this was never seen by King John as by October 1216 he had died of dysentery at the age of just 50.

But by this time the great Charters had achieved a great deal of popularity and had acquired heritage, it had been shown that the Charters could be used as leverage and justification to bring a reluctant king to Runnymede to seal into law, articles and clauses concerning liberties, which we now call 'freedom and democracy'. Once these ideas of freedom had been liberated by the events of June 1215 and it had been shown that not even the king was above the law of the land, the "Magna Carta" became a document and idea that could never be changed or un-written.

Once sealed, up to thirteen copies of the 'Magna Carta' were quickly distributed throughout the country to great Cathedrals. In today's terms, the "Magna Carta" had gone viral and there was no stopping it. There were too many witnesses to the sealing of the document, some bishops themselves, for the 'Magna Carta' to ever be forgotten or denied.

And during the next 800 years, the "Magna Carta" became a great authority in respect of the central key clauses usually referred to as 38 and 39, these have not only stood the test of time against hundreds of attempts to annul, repeal, or modify by successive monarchs and governments but are still the basis of 'Freedom and Democracy' today.

The 'Magna Carta' has also been exported to many countries throughout the world, one of the greatest adoptions of the 'Magna Carta' can be seen in the American Constitution, which carries the same cause of 'Freedom and Liberty' to all.

Who signed the 'Magna Carta'? There were 25 signatures in all as listed below.

'Surety Barons for the enforcement of Magna Carta':

1.   William d'Aubigny, Lord of Belvoir Castle.
2.   Roger Bigod, Earl of Norfolk and Suffolk.
3.   Hugh Bigod, Heir to the Earldoms of Norfolk and Suffolk.
4.   Henry de Bohun, Earl of Hereford.
5.   Richard de Clare, Earl of Hertford.
6.   Gilbert de Clare, heir to the Earldom of Hertford.
7.   John FitzRobert, Lord of Warkworth Castle.
8.   Robert Fitzwalter, Lord of Dunmow Castle.
9.   William de Fortibus, Earl of Albemarle.
10.   William Hardel, **Mayor of the City of London.
11.   William de Huntingfield, Sheriff of Norfolk and Suffolk.
12.   John de Lacy, Lord of Pontefract Castle.
13.   William de Lavallee, Lord of Stanway Castle.
14.   William Malet, Sheriff of Somerset and Dorset.
15.   Geoffrey de Mandeville, Earl of Essex and Gloucester.
16.   William Marshall Jr, heir to the Earldom of Pembroke.
17.   Roger de Montbegon, Lord of Hornby Castle, Lancashire.
18.   Richard de Montfichet, Baron.
19.   William de Mowbray, Lord of Axholme Castle.
20.   Richard de Percy, Baron.
21.   Saire/Saher de Quincy, Earl of Winchester.
22.   Robert de Roos, Lord of Ham Lake Castle.
23.   Geoffrey de Saye, Baron.
24.   Robert de Vere, heir to the Earldom of Oxford.
25.   Eustace de Vesci, Lord of Alnwick Castle.

By the sheer amount of dignitaries and those in high office signing the document, it can be seen how popular and what absolute respect was given to The "Magna Carta", and it's legacy, has remained strong for 800 years, it also gave inspiration to Simon de Montfort to elect the first English Parliament in 1264. The English civil war saw more drastic conclusions to the monarch's powers and authority, but it was the spirit of the "Magna Carta" though that evoked the Putney debates of 1647. With the Restoration of Charles II, the "Magna Carta" helped to codify the ancient writ of Habeas Corpus that was passed by parliament in 1679.

Indeed, the European Convention of Human Rights echoes the "Magna Carta" in Article 6, and many people in Europe and beyond have inherited the events of June 1215.

Pre-1300c Monarchs

Who were the Monarchs of the 11th and 12th century then, before King John and the signing of the "Magna Carta" in the 13c that had led to the unrest within the country, below you can see that there were 5 Kings and one Queen between 1056 and 1199 when John came to the throne.

William II (Rufus) (c.1056 - 1100) Photo ©

Known as William Rufus because of his ruddy complexion, he was the third son of William the Conqueror (William I) and inherited the English throne from him.

William was born in around 1056 and almost nothing is known about his childhood. At his death in 1087, William I bequeathed his original inheritance, the Duchy of Normandy, to his eldest son, Robert Curthose. He gave England to William, his third and a favourite son, who was crowned in September 1087. In 1088, William faced a baronial rebellion inspired by his uncle, Odo of Bayeux, in favour of Robert. But Robert failed to appear and the revolt soon collapsed. In 1089, he laid claim to Normandy and waged war against Robert, who he defeated and reduced to a subordinate role. In 1096, Robert went on Crusade, mortgaging Normandy to William (for 10,000 marks), who raised the money by levying a heavy and much, resented! tax in England.

William faced opposition from Scotland and in 1091 he compelled Malcolm III, King of the Scots to acknowledge his overlordship. Malcolm revolted in November 1093, but William's forces crushed his army near Alnwick and Malcolm was killed. Thereafter, William maintained the Scottish kings as vassals.

William also had difficult relations with the church. He kept bishoprics vacant to make use of their revenues, and had numerous arguments with Anselm, Archbishop of Canterbury from 1093. When Anselm left for Rome in 1097 to seek the advice of the Pope, William seized his estates.

On 2 August 1100, William died when he was shot by an arrow while out hunting. It was accepted as an accident but could have been an assassination. It has been suggested that his alleged slayer, Walter Tyrel, was acting under orders from William's younger brother, Henry, who promptly seized the throne as Henry I.

Henry 1st 1100 to 1135, Photo ©

Henry the 1st was the youngest and most able of William the Conqueror's sons, Henry strengthened the crown's executive powers and modernised royal administration.

Henry was born in England in 1068 or 1069, the fourth son of William the Conqueror. By the time his elder brother William became king, one of Henry's other older brothers had died, leaving Robert as the only other potential successor. William was killed in a hunting accident in August 1100, and Henry had himself crowned a few days later, taking advantage of Robert's absence on crusade. With a number of barons supporting Robert, however, Henry's succession was precarious. He moved quickly to buy support by granting favours, abolishing abuses and making wide-ranging concessions in his Charter of Liberties. In November 1100, he married Edith, sister of the king of Scotland, in order to secure his northern border. When Robert invaded England in 1101 Henry, with some popular and baronial support, agreed on an amicable settlement. Robert relinquished his claim in return for Henry's territories in Normandy and a large annuity. But his chaotic reign of Normandy prompted Henry to invade. He routed Robert's army at Tinchebrai in 1106, capturing Robert and holding him prisoner for life.

Henry's frequent absences from England prompted the development of a bureaucracy that could operate effectively in his absence. His reign marked a significant advance from personal monarchy towards the bureaucratized state of the future. The Exchequer was developed to deal with royal revenues, royal justices began to tour the shire's to reinforce local administration and inquire into revenues, often aggressively.

Abroad, his possessions in Normandy were challenged by Robert's son, William Clito. Henry was obliged to repel two assaults by Clito's supporters and Norman barons who resented Henry's officials and high taxes. By 1120, however, the barons had submitted, Henry's only legitimate son William had been married to the daughter of the powerful Count of Anjou and Louis VI of France had agreed terms for peace after defeat in battle.

In November 1120, Henry's son died in a shipwreck, from then on the question of the succession dominated the politics of his reign. Henry summoned his only other legitimate child Matilda back to England, made his barons pay homage to her as his heir. In 1128, Matilda was married to Geoffrey Plantagenet another member of the Angevin family. English barons did not want to be ruled by a woman and an Angevin and on Henry's death in December 1135, there was a succession crisis which led to civil war.

King Stephen (1135 - 1154), Photo ©

King of England from 1135. He was the grandson of William the Conqueror and came to the throne in 1135, although he had previously recognized Henry I's daughter Matilda as heiress to the throne. Matilda landed in England in 1139, and civil war disrupted the country with fighting between Stephen and forces loyal to Matilda. Stephen was briefly taken prisoner and Matilda declared Queen until she was defeated at the Battle of Farringdon in 1145. In 1153, Stephen acknowledged Matilda's son, Henry II, as his own heir.

In 1135 Steven usurps the throne from Matilda, King Henry's Daughter, but a year later the Earl of Norfolk leads a rebellion against Stephen starting a civil war known as 'The Anarchy' war. In 1138 Robert Earl of Gloucester son of Henry I, deserts Stephen and pledges allegiance to Matilda, David I of Scotland, Matilda's uncle invades England to support Matilda but is stopped at Northallerton, in 1139 Matilda leaves France for England and in 1141, Matilda's forces overthrew Stephen at the battle of Lincoln, Matilda is proclaimed queen, Earl Robert is taken prisoner in exchange for Stephens release. In 1145 Stephens's forces defeat Matilda's forces at the battle of Faringdon, Matilda abandons her cause and returns to France.

Matilda (1102 - 1167) Artist's impression of Matilda, Picture ©

Matilda was born in 1102, the daughter of Henry I King of England. In 1114, she married the Holy Roman Emperor Henry V. The death of Matilda's brother in 1120 made her Henry I sole legitimate heir. When her husband died in 1125, Henry recalled her to England and, in 1127, he insisted that the nobles accept her as his successor. In 1128, she married Geoffrey of Anjou with whom she had three sons. A woman ruler was unprecedented and her marriage to Geoffrey was unpopular. When Henry I died in 1135 Matilda's cousin Stephen of Blois immediately had himself crowned king.

Though the church and most nobles supported Stephen, Matilda's claims were upheld by her half-brother Robert of Gloucester and her uncle David I of Scotland. Matilda and Robert landed at Arundel in September 1139 and England descended into civil war. The war was used as a cover for the settling of local feuds, leaving much of the country in anarchy.

Henry II (1133 - 1189) Henry II, Photo ©

King of England from 1154 Henry strengthened royal administration but suffered from quarrels with Thomas Becket and his own family.

Henry was born at Le Mans in North West France on 4 March 1133. His father was Count of Anjou and his mother Matilda, daughter of Henry I of England. Henry had named Matilda as his successor to the English throne but her cousin Stephen had taken over.

In 1150 - 1151, Henry became ruler of Normandy and Anjou after the death of his father. In 1152, he married Eleanor of Aquitaine, the greatest heiress in Western Europe. In 1153, he crossed to England to pursue his claim to the throne, reaching an agreement that he would succeed Stephen on his death which occurred in 1154.

Henry now began to restore order. Using his talented Chancellor Thomas Becket, Henry began reorganising the judicial system. The Assize of Clarendon (1166) established procedures of criminal justice, establishing courts and prisons for those awaiting trial. In addition, the assizes gave fast and clear verdicts, enriched the treasury and extended royal control.

In 1164, Henry reasserted his ancestral rights over the church. Now Archbishop of Canterbury Thomas Becket refused to comply, an attempted reconciliation failed and Becket punished priests who had co-operated with Henry. On hearing this Henry reportedly exclaimed, 'Will no one rid me of this turbulent priest?' four knights took his words literally and murdered Becket in Canterbury Cathedral in December 1170. Almost overnight Becket became a saint. Henry reconciled himself with the church, but royal control over the church changed little.

In 1169, an Anglo-Norman force landed in Ireland to support of one of the claimants to the Irish high kingship. Fearing the creation of a separate Norman power to the West, Henry travelled to Dublin to assert his overlordship of the territory they had won. So, an English presence in Ireland was established. In the course of his reign, Henry had dominion over territories stretching from Ireland to the Pyrenees.

Henry now had problems within his own family. His sons - Henry, Geoffrey, Richard, and John - mistrusted each other and resented their father's policy of dividing land among them. There were serious family disputes in 1173, 1181 and 1184. The king's attempt to find an inheritance for John led to opposition from Richard and Philip II of France. Henry was forced to give way. The news, that, John had also turned against him, hastened Henry's death on 6 July 1189.

Richard I (1157 - 1199) Richard I, Photo ©

Richard was born on 8 September 1157 in Oxford, son of Henry II and Eleanor of Aquitaine. He possessed considerable political and military ability. However, like his brothers, he fought with his family, joining them in the great rebellion against their father in 1173. In 1183, his brother Henry died, leaving Richard, heir to the throne. Henry II wanted to give Aquitaine to his youngest son, John. Richard refused and in 1189 joined forces with Philip II of France against his father, hounding him to a premature death in July 1189.

As, king, Richard's chief ambition was to join the Third Crusade, prompted by Saladin's capture of Jerusalem in 1187. To finance this, he sold Sheriffdoms and other offices and in 1190 he departed for the Holy Land. In May, he reached Cyprus where he married Berengaria, daughter of the king of Navarre. Richard arrived in the Holy Land in June 1191 and Acre fell the following month.

In September, his victory at Arsuf gave the Crusaders possession of Joppa. Although he came close, Jerusalem the crusades main objective eluded him. Moreover, fierce quarrels among the French, German and English contingents provided further troubles. After a year's stalemate, Richard made a truce with Saladin and started his journey home.

Bad weather drove him ashore near Venice and he was imprisoned by Duke Leopold of Austria before being handed over to the German Emperor Henry VI, who ransomed him for the huge sum of 150,000 marks. The raising of the ransom was a remarkable achievement in February 1194.

Richard was released. He returned at once to England and was crowned for a second time, fearing that the ransom payment had compromised his independence. Yet a month later he went to Normandy, never to return. His last five years were spent in intermittent warfare against Philip II.

While besieging the castle of Châlus in central France, he was fatally wounded and died on 6 April 1199. He was succeeded by his younger brother John, who had spent the years of Richard's absence scheming against him.

John (c.1167 - 1216) John I, Photo ©

John was a king of England who is most famous for signing

*the **'Magna Carta'.***

John was born around Christmas in 1166 or 1167 in Oxford, the youngest and a favourite son of Henry II. On his father's death, in 1189 his brother Richard became king. John received titles lands and money, but this was not enough. In October 1190, Richard recognised his nephew Arthur as his heir. Three years later, when Richard was imprisoned in Germany, John tried to seize control. He was unsuccessful and when Richard returned in early 1194 was banished. The two were soon reconciled and when Arthur was captured by Philip II in 1196, Richard named John, his heir.

In 1199, Richard died and John became king. War with France was renewed triggered by John's second marriage. When asked to mediate between the rival families of Lusignan and Angoulâme, he married the Angoulâme heiress Isabella, who had been betrothed to Hugh de Lusignan. A rebellion broke out and John was ordered to appear before his overlord Philip II of France. His failure to do so resulted in war.

By 1206, John had lost Normandy, Anjou, Maine and parts of Poitou. These failures were a damaging blow to his prestige and he was determined to win them back. This required money, so his government became increasingly ruthless and efficient in its financial administration, taxes soared and he began to exploit his feudal rights ever more harshly.

This bred increasing Baronial discontent, negotiations between John and his Barons failed and civil war broke out in May 1215. When the rebels seized London, John was compelled to negotiate further, on 19 June at Runnymede on the River Thames, he accepted the Baronial terms embodied in the 'Magna Carta', which limited royal power, ensured feudal rights and reinstated English law. It was the first formal document stating that the Monarch was as much under the rule of law as his people and that the rights of individuals were to be upheld even against the wishes of the sovereign.

This settlement was soon rendered impractical when John claimed it was signed under duress. Pope Innocent took his side and in the ensuing civil war, John laid waste to the northern counties and the Scottish border. Prince Louis of France then invaded at the Barons' request. John continued to wage war vigorously, but his death in October 1216 enabled a compromise, peace and the succession of his son Henry III.

From the list of pre 13th century monarch's it can be seen that they lived relatively short lives and were constantly embroiled in battles for the power to rule, often with their own families, such was the distrust of the times.

What were the typical dressing fashions of the 13ᵗʰ Century?

Lincolnshire. There is a strong link to the 'Magna Carta' and Lincolnshire, St Hugh was not the only Bishop of Lincoln to influence the course of 'Magna Carta' history. His successor, Bishop Hugh of Wells, was one of the original signatories at 'Runnymede' and as such his name appears on the 1215 charter. That Bishop Hugh of Wells was influential enough to present the king with such a charter illustrates the position of Lincolnshire as a major centre of political power in the 13th century. These names represent a 'who's who' of the political powers in early 13th century England.

Indeed, so that the charter's terms were known throughout the kingdom, contemporary copies were drawn up and sent to great seats of power within each county. Such a copy was sent to the Bishop of Lincoln, who kept it at Lincoln Cathedral. Amazingly, it appears not to have been moved and has remained in place for almost 800 years. One of the only four known 1215 copies, the Lincoln 'Magna Carta' is on permanent display at Lincoln Castle except for brief periods when it is taken on a tour overseas.

Magna Carta' and the Battle of Lincoln Fair

Civil war in England did not end at Runnymede. When in October 1216 King John died of dysentery at Lincoln's castle. Shown below.

The Kingdom was in turmoil. Advisors to the new King Henry III realised the importance of bringing peace to the Kingdom and saw the charter as a vital part of this process.

Lincoln Castle, one of the two remaining royalist strongholds, was to play a pivotal role at the end of the civil war and the development of 1215 Charter into the 'Magna Carta' we recognise today. Under siege from the rebel barons' forces, Lincoln Castle had so far held out in a spirited defense led by Lincolnshire's very own female constable Nicolaa de la Haye.

A decisive battle was fought in May 1217 when William Marshall, Earl of Pembroke, led royalist forces to aid the stout-hearted constable, and the siege was ended at the Battle of Lincoln Fair. Following this decisive victory a council was held and the Charter of 1215 was reissued in the name of Henry III. The young king's advisors hoped that by reaffirming the rights of the people and the limits of the king's power the Kingdom might finally be restored to peace. And so 'Magna Carta' as we know it today came into being.

Charter of the Forest

It was at this time that clauses relating to the unjust and harsh system of 'Forest Law' were removed from the 1215 Charter to be given expression in a separate document known as 'Charter of the Forest'. This copy of 'Charter of the Forest' is one of only two known to have survived. It is on permanent display at Lincoln Castle. Under King John, certain rights allowing people to make their living off the land were being eroded by the King as he took common land and made it his own private 'Royal Forest'. Anyone found hunting or allowing their animals to graze in 'Royal Forest' was subject to severe penalties that could lead to bodily dismemberment or even death. 'Charter of the Forest' reduced these penalties and claimed back common land from the crown. From 1217, the Charter of 1215 became known as 'Magna Carta', or 'The Grand Charter', and was subsequently reissued on several occasions, always alongside the 'Charter of the Forest'.

The Legacy of 'Magna Carta'

From its very beginnings, 'Magna Carta' has been the focus of fierce negotiations over accountability, power, and justice. Over the centuries, countless people engaged in struggles with governments and leaders have called on 'The Charter' to justify their rights and liberties. The right to due process and trial by jury, the right of the people to petition their leaders, and the development of Parliaments as a barrier to the excessive power of the Monarch, have all been heavily influenced by the clauses first set out in 'Magna Carta'.

The significance of 'Magna Carta' is felt throughout the world. Many nations have adopted its principles in the pursuit of democracy and still more look to it as a beacon of justice. With such a strong role in its development, Lincolnshire can proudly recognise 'Magna Carta' as an iconic part of the county's heritage.

What does 'Magna Carta' say?

'For a trivial offence, a free man shall be fined only in proportion to the degree of his offence, and for a serious offence correspondingly, but not so heavily as to deprive him of his livelihood....None of these fines shall be imposed except by the assessment on oath of reputable men of the neighbourhood.'

'No man shall be forced to perform more service for a knight's 'fee', or another free holding of land than is due from it.'

'No constable or another royal official shall take corn or other movable goods from any man without immediate payment, unless the seller voluntarily offers postponement of this.'

'SINCE WE HAVE GRANTED ALL THESE THINGS for God, for the better ordering of our kingdom, and to allay the discord that has arisen between us and our Barons, and since we desire that they shall be enjoyed in their entirety, with lasting strength forever, we give and grant to the Barons the following security: The Barons shall elect twenty-five of their number to keep and cause to be observed with all their might, the peace and liberties granted and confirmed to them by this Charter'

What does 'Charter of the Forest' say?

'Henceforth, no one shall lose life or limbs on account of our hunting rights; but if anyone is arrested and convicted of taking our venison, let him redeem himself by a heavy payment if he has anything with which to redeem himself. And if he has nothing with which to redeem himself, let him lie in our prison for a year and a day. And if, after the year and the day, he can find sureties, let him be freed from prison; but if he cannot, let him abjure the realm of England'

'Henceforth every Freeman, in his wood or on his land that he has in the forest, may with impunity make a mill, fish-preserve, pond, marl-pit, ditch, or arable in cultivated land outside covers, provided that no injury is thereby given to any neighbour'

'Every freeman may in his own Woods have eyries of hawks, sparrow hawks, falcons, eagles, and herons, and he may also have honey that is found in his Woods.

This was then a great end to the ruling of the land by the Monarch's and freedom from their repression.

We cannot leave the Lincolnshire connection though without first looking at the link

with the 'Magna Carta' to the small village of **Epworth** in the northern part of the county, known as the Isle of Axholme, for it, was here that William de Mowbray, Lord of Axholme Castle, and one of the 25 signatories and witnesses to the signing of the 'Magna Carta' lived, the castle fell into ruin and all, that is left now, is a circular mound of earth where the castle once stood.

<< Axholme Castle

The Mobray Arms Public House stands near the Old Rectory Museum in the Village of Epworth in the Isle of Axholme N.Lincolnshire

The Mowbray Arms Public House

William de Mowbray had lived in Epworth close to St Andrews Church in the village, there is also a book about the de Mowbray family written by Marilyn Roberts called 'The Mowbray Legacy' well worth reading with the full history of the de Mowbray family documented.

Epworth and the Wesleyan Church Connection

The Old Rectory

St Andrew Church

This little Gem of a village tucked away in the heart of the English countryside is also the Birth Place of John and Charles Wesley, the founder of the Methodist Church.

There is also a fine Memorial Church to John and Charles Wesley and the Rectory, that was their home dating back to 1709, is now the Old Rectory Museum, the original building was rebuilt after it burnt down, it is suspected that this fire was an act of arson perpetrated by opponents of John and Charles Wesley.

I am very proud to have family connections with the town of Epworth my mother being born there and grandfather a preacher in the village.

We have looked in some detail then at one of probably the most important things to come from the early 13th Century the signing of the 'Magna Carta', but what else was in news from this era.

We mentioned in the first paragraph about the start of two of England's great institutions that had their beginnings in the early part of the 1200c they were the Oxford and Cambridge universities.

Intellectuals started gathered in the town of Oxford to create a place of learning and development as early as 1100', and by early 1200's learning houses had developed, It grew rapidly from 1167 when Henry II banned English students from attending the University of Paris. After disputes between students and Oxford townsfolk in 1209, some academics fled northeast to Cambridge, where they established what was to become the University of Cambridge. The two ancient universities are frequently jointly referred to as "Oxbridge".

The University is made up from a variety of institutions, including 38 constituent colleges and a full range of academic departments which are organised into four divisions. All the colleges are self-governing institutions as part of the University, each controlling its own membership and with its own internal structure and activities, being a city university, it does not have a campus; instead, all the buildings and facilities are scattered throughout the metropolitan centre.

1209

Groups of scholars congregate at the ancient Roman trading post of Cambridge for the purpose of, study, the earliest record of the University.

1284

Peterhouse, the first college at Cambridge, is founded by the Bishop of Ely.

1347

Mary, Countess of Pembroke, founds Pembroke College.

1446

Henry VI, founder of Eton and of King's College, Cambridge, lays the first stone of King's College Chapel.

1503

Thomas Cranmer, aged 14, enters the newly endowed Jesus College.

1511

Lady Margaret Beaufort, mother of Henry VII, founds St John's College.

1516

Erasmus, Lady Margaret Professor of Divinity at Cambridge, works on the translation of the Greek New Testament and on textbooks which were to become the staple of the 'new learning'. His work led to him being considered the most important scholar of the Northern Renaissance.

1533

Thomas Cranmer ends his career in Cambridge to become the first post-reformation Archbishop of Canterbury. While in the post, he annuls Henry VIII's marriages to Catherine of Aragon and Anne Boleyn and divorces him from Anne of Cleves. He is also largely responsible for the Book of Common Prayer, the official directory of worship of the Church of England.

1546

Henry VIII founds Trinity College, Cambridge.

1584

The Cambridge University Press, the world's oldest established press, begins its unbroken record of publishing every year until the present.

1600

Dr William Gilbert of St John's publishes his 'De Magnete', a scientific work fundamental to the development of navigation and map making.

Chronology of facts from 1087 to 1326

1087 William the Conqueror dies - William Rufus
becomes King of England
Robert becomes II Duke of Normandy.

1088 Odo of Bayeaux challenged by William Rufus
on Robert's behalf

1093 Donald III Bane, King of Scots

1097 Edgar, King of Scots

1100 William Rufus dies - Henry I becomes King of
England

1101 Treaty of Alton confirms Henry I as King of
England Robert as Duke of
Normandy

1106 Henry I defeats Robert at Tinchebrai and
becomes Duke of Normandy

1107 Alexander I becomes King of Scotland

1120 Henry I son and heir drown's, Matilda is
heiress

1124 David I becomes King of Scotland

1128 Matilda marries Geoffrey of Anjou

1135 Stephen I becomes King of England

1138 Civil war begins. David, I of Scots, invades England Robert of Gloucester
supports Matilda's claim

1139 Matilda arrives in England

1141 Matilda and Robert of Gloucester defeat
Stephen at Lincoln

1145 Stephen is victorious at Farringdon

1152 Henry Plantagenet marries Eleanor of
Aquitaine

1153 Malcolm IV, King of Scots and Henry
Plantagenet recognized as Stephen's
heir

1154 Stephen dies - Henry II becomes King and
Nicholas Breakspear becomes Pope Adrian
IV

1155 Henry receives 'papal bull' to conquer and
rule Ireland

1162 Thomas Becket becomes archbishop of Canterbury

1164 Constitutions of Clarendon are issued

1165 William I, the Lion, of Scots

1170 Richard de Clare invades Ireland

1177 Henry II's youngest son, John, is made Lord of Ireland

1183 Henry the Young King dies

1189 Henry is defeated by his son Richard and
Philip II Augustus of France Richard I, the Lionheart becomes king

1190 Richard joined the Third Crusade

1192 Richard is imprisoned in Germany

1194 Richard returns to England1199   Richard dies while fighting in France - John I become King of England

1200 John makes peace with France and marries Isabel of Angouleme

1203 Arthur of Brittany is murdered

1204 John loses French territories to Philip Augustus of France

1207 John refuses to accept Stephen Langton as Archbishop of Canterbury Papal interdict is imposed on England

1213 John offers the Pope England as a fiefdom

1214 Alexander II, King of Scots

1215 Barons force John to accept 'Magna Carta.'

1216 John dies - Henry III becomes King of England William the Marshal becomes Regent

1217 Louis VIII defeated at the Battle of Lincoln

1219 William the Marshal dies

1221 Alexander II, king of Scots, marries Joan, daughter of King John

1236 Henry III marries Eleanor of Provence

1238 Simon de Montfort marries Henry III sister, Eleanor

1249 Alexander III, king of Scots

1258 Provisions of Oxford

1259 Provisions of Westminster

1264 Second Barons' War

1265 De Montfort dies at Battle of Evesham

1271 Henry III dies - Edward I becomes king and Marco Polo goes to China

1272 Henry III dies - Edward I becomes king

1274 Edward returns from his Crusade and is crowned King

1277 Edward begins his campaign in Wales

1282 Llewellyn, Prince of North Wales, dies at Builth

1283 Edward I conquers Wales, Statute of Wales

1290 Edward expels Jews from England

1291 Edward arbitrates over Scottish succession

1292 John Balliol, King of Scots

1296 Edward begins his campaign in Scotland

1306 Robert I, the Bruce, King of Scotland

1307 Edward I dies - Edward II becomes King

1314 English defeated at Bannockburn

1318 Edward II regains England and the Despensers rise to power

1322 Edward II defeats the Marcher Lords and the Lancastrians Thomas of
     Lancaster is executed

1326 Queen Isabella and Mortimer invade England

By the 14th-Century things, were changing

The 1370s brought other social and economic problems, Landlords and their peasant tenants were set against each other because economic change had made the social structure of the 12th and early 13th century become outdated.

The thirteenth century was an era of great expansion, population, agricultural production, commercial activity, and prices for commodities had all been rising since the eleventh and twelve century. Landlords had done very well. Land was scarce and labour was plentiful. Thus, prices for their agricultural produce and rents for their properties were high, while wages were low. There was profit to be made in exploiting the rights most Lords held over their peasant neighbours.

Management by literate professional farmers became normal on the big estates, and some of the lesser ones, an era of high yield intensive farming followed, supervised by the wealthy Landowners and Landlords of the time.

After 1315, this pattern was disturbed. 1315 was the beginning of the first major famine England and Western Europe had seen in a long time. Many people who had been living at the bare subsistence level died. Thereafter the population continued to decline, perhaps because peasants began to marry later and limit the size of their families. The great expansion of the 13th century had come to an end. A long recession, in which markets shrank and prices fell, had started.

The greatest single blow to England was the Black Death (bubonic plague) of 1348-49, its estimated this may have killed up to a third of the England's population. It is difficult to imagine the devastation of this catastrophe, the plague, following on from the earlier decline and recession had changed the shape of society completely. The prosperity of the earlier period was based on expansion. The upper classes in particular had benefited from their ownership of scarce resources and the cheapness of labour. By the second half of the 14th century, labour became the scarcest resource, while everything else, dropped, in price. Food and other agricultural commodities became cheaper because the market for them was smaller. Rents were lower, the return on land was less and there were fewer people competing for it.

The new economic climate spelled opportunity for the peasant survivors of the plague. This situation frightened the landlords. Their income was falling at precisely the time that wages were soaring, almost immediately in 1349, the king's council issued an ordinance forbidding wage raises. In 1351, Parliament passed its first notable economic legislation the 'Statute of Labourers'.

Wages were fixed at the pre-plague levels, and all landless men under sixty were compelled to accept work, and a man's own Lord had first claim on his services at those rates. Agricultural workers were forbidden to leave their masters before their contracts ended, and no other person was to hire them if they did.

Workers increasingly resented the lords. They were not short of land or work as their ancestors had been in the past, they knew they could manage on their own, out of such perceived injustice came revolutionary ideas. The peasants revolted and refused to work for their lords.

The situation in the 1370s

The conflict with the peasants added tensions in the 1370s. The landlord classes, to which almost all taxpayers belonged, was being squeezed from above and below at the same time. Their discomfort led to an attempt to change the taxation system to give them some relief at the expense of the poor.

Such was their demise that the landowners, who sat in parliament, decided there must be a better way to raise money. They tried taxes on the Church, and they were even trying taxes on the laity. Thus in 1377, ahead or poll tax was devised, every lay person over the age of 14 was to pay 4 pence, a lot of money for a poor person in those days.

It was a very unpopular tax. The thought of everyone, rich or poor, paying the same amount of tax bothered many people, taxpayers got annoyed by tax collectors constantly querying them about their personal circumstances. This did not bother parliamentarians, they were more worried that the tax was not bringing in the revenue they had expected, and so, in 1379 a graduated poll tax was introduced. The fact that the rich were paying more did not stop the unease of parliament as the tax was still yielding less than Parliament and the King's council had hoped for.

As the financial crisis had worsened by the following year 1380, Parliament went ahead with a further poll tax change, once again rich and poor were to pay the same, but the tax rate was raised and by 1381, every person above the age of 15 was to pay one shilling (12 pence), three times the rate of the first poll tax of 1377.

Parliament was not oblivious to the fact that this was impossible for the poor to pay, an average family income was around 20 shillings a year or less, a family with two adults would have to pay ten percent of their yearly income in taxes.

Parliamentarians were sure that the rich would help the poor to pay out of decency and instructions were given to tax collectors to collect the tax in two instalments, this did nothing to stem public discontent. People refused to cooperate with the tax collectors, and up to a third of the adult population succeeded in avoiding the tax.

The London tax collectors reported to the Exchequer that they could not do their job without stirring up a dangerous situation. The King's council simply told collectors to collect the whole tax at once, this was a fatal mistake. In June of 1381, commissioners following the instructions of their superiors sparked an uprising in Brentwood in Essex.

The Peasants' Revolt of 1381

Essex, along with Kent and East Anglia, were areas where the unfair taxes was felt the most. These county's had small free and near-free landholders, well placed to take advantage of good economic conditions, they resented the harassment being placed on them by lords who were trying to enforce their remaining right on them.

The poll tax was the last straw for these southeastern villagers, there were no great men in residence who might see an obligation to help meet the local tax bill. Everyone was in the same economic position, and equally in danger of financial ruin. It was these villagers with common interests that came together to defy outsiders.

The uprising spread rapidly throughout the Essex villages. Quite independently there was also a tax revolt in Kent. The two peasant armies soon got together and converged on London to make their demands known on parliament. Despite the upper-classes being against the peasants, the peasants had a good political understanding, and their view of the current political situation was much the same as the knights who sat in Parliament.

Peasants were also angry about military failures. The war was going so badly that the coast suffered constant raids from French and Castilian ships. When the men of Kent marched on London, they left everyone living near the sea to defend the coast. Not to have done so would have left the country helpless before its foreign enemies.

Peasants were angry about the financial crisis. They, like parliamentarians, believed that corruption was behind the problem. The men of Essex chose the property of the royal treasurer to be pillaged, they told the monks at Canterbury to elect one of their own to be archbishop, because the current one, a royal chancellor, was a traitor and they were on their way to London to behead him.

The amount of the peasant dissatisfaction and the belief of the peasants that they could do something about the problems themselves was a remarkable aspect of the peasant revolts of 1381. More uprisings took place as the peasants took it upon themselves to demand freedom from their oppressive ecclesiastical landlords.

The peasant groups quickly converged on London. And the young King Richard II (14 years old) was forced to act, he negotiated with the two rebel groups from Essex and Kent personally, as they camped on opposite sides of the Thames outside of London.

The Essex men dispersed as Richard II promised them 'Charters of emancipation', which showed that most rebels were willing to settle for less. Wyatt Tyler, the leader from Kent, wanted more, but he had overplayed his hand, and was killed.

At that moment, Richard II coolly declared to the rebels "I am your leader" and this prevented a massacre. They dispersed and went home. Once the threat in London was over, the government was free to restore the 'status quo ante'. But none of the promises made by the king were ever kept.

The Results of the Peasants Revolt

The only effects the peasant's revolt had then was that Poll taxes fell out of use.

Otherwise, it made almost no difference to the long-term economic or social development in England.

We can see from this that the signing of the Magna Carta brought Freedom, Democracy, Human Rights and released from repression to England and beyond.

Otherwise, little has changed in the last 800 years, we have come through the industrial revolution, seen great technological advances and better health care for all, but we are still fighting wars, still appealing against increased taxes levied on us, and in many cases still fighting poverty.

It would be interesting to see what will happen over the next 800 years, and what will have changed, if anything?.

www.ingramcontent.com/pod-product-compliance
Lightning Source LLC
Chambersburg PA
CBHW072024290526
45787CB00014B/1875